EVERYTHING
FROM
NOTHING

Why There Is Anything
And How There Is Purpose

I0158702

S. E. ELWELL

PressCore
PUBLISHING

CONTENTS

INTRODUCTION

Science continues to push the boundaries of our understanding of nature and the universe. Yet despite all the discoveries and breakthroughs, we are still left wondering why it all exists in the first place. Why is there anything at all rather than just absolutely nothing? This age-old question has captivated the minds of philosophers and physicists for centuries.

Various theories have been suggested, ranging from the possibility of an ultimate "uncaused cause" to the idea that existence is simply a mathematical necessity. But still, an overriding question persists: — is there any ultimate purpose or meaning to it all? If so, what? And how does consciousness fit in? Could there be some form of a continuation or ascension of consciousness? If so, where? And how?

These profound questions beg answers, even if it is common in this scientific era to dismiss any such deeper meaning as non-scientific. This antipathy to a *grand purpose* is probably due to the cold mechanical facts of *materialism* that merely reduce matter to its most basic components. However, this book offers perspectives that can dispel this glum conclusion by postulating logical arguments (still based on science-friendly facts) to show how there is likely far more positive potential than we can currently see. By this, I mean that the ultimate source of all existence is **attracted to positivity** and away from negativity on a scale far beyond what we can empirically observe — and the evolution of consciousness is intrinsic to this whole multidimensional process.

Therefore, should you ever wonder if it is still realistic to believe in a higher purpose even in this modern science-educated age, I propose that the answer is an emphatic YES. In this book, I will describe some of these arguments based on a modern-day understanding of the physical universe and taking into account credible metaphysical and philosophical perspectives and insights.

I hope you will find this book enlightening, eye-opening, and uplifting, whatever your current beliefs might be.

Chapter One

WHY ANYTHING AT ALL?

Where did the universe come from, and why? These huge questions are crying out for an explanation, especially when many people around the world are turning away from religion in favor of assuming that modern scientific research will provide answers.

People place confidence and trust in science because it is questioning, scrutinizing, or analytical. Research within science is open and inquisitive rather than dogmatic and closed. Its discoveries are not based on presumptions but on verifiable facts and confirmed observations. What's more, this analytical scrutiny has guided our knowledge and understanding of nature so astonishingly far that many people assume there are no boundaries to what science can explain — all without the need for positing the existence of a *Creator*.

However, there is a problem.

As we learn more and more about the universe, it is getting more and more difficult to put the reason for its creation down to mere chance. Even those most skeptical of *intelligent design* must acknowledge this fact. Many laws of nature are so astonishingly fine-tuned it seems absurd to account for them as merely good luck. And the further we go into this evaluation of the universe, the more coincidences we need to dismiss as an unthinkably massive dose of good fortune — far too much and too many for most people to accept without concluding that there must be another explanation behind it all.

...But what?

One possible answer is that there could be many, or perhaps even an infinite number of other universes (*multiverse theory*). And if this is true, and there are an unlimited number of alternative or parallel dimensions or separate realms of reality, each could have its own natural order or determined laws. Therefore, our extraordinary life-producing universe is possible because it happens to have this order established just right.

However, there still has to be a reason for all this too. The multiple universes must come from somewhere or have arisen from some fundamental origin. So why has this ultimate *first cause* worked things out so that, at the very least, one universe is sufficiently stable and well-ordered enough to support life?

Such questions open up the suggestion that there must be an intelligence at the bottom of it all. However, this is seen as unscientific because it does not explain what created this intelligence. In other words, we need to know the nature of this intelligence and where this mentality came from. And if the answer is God, then what created God? In this modern-day science-led world, many people want to feel any talk of a *Supreme Being* or *higher power* is based on valid arguments rather than just blind faith.

My aim is to explore naturalistic perspectives on why there is anything in existence at all, leading logically to how there is purpose, all without the need to follow any particular religious doctrine. To do this, I will adhere to a modern understanding of the fundamental aspects of nature and argue a point of view that, hopefully, most people can accept is in concordance with facts and reason.

ULTIMATE ORIGIN

First, let's state the obvious. There is a lot more than absolutely nothing. There is the whole universe for a start, not to mention the possibility of multiple universes. Therefore, it stands to reason that the **potential** for all this *creation* must have always existed **before** anything could materialize in reality. But where did this underlying potential come from, and why has it gone to so much trouble to create at least one cosmos?

By "cosmos," of course, we are talking about an orderly, harmonious system of space and time and the energy and matter that make up the properties of our universe. Why would, and indeed, how could it all emerge (as some scientists suggest) from absolutely nothing? This premise seems implausible. Logic dictates that there must be some underlying **source**. But where did this source come from? And where did that source's source come from? We could continue asking this question forever. Eventually, we must accept that the universe is part of something that is somehow **infinite**, whether we can imagine this or not. And we can't. So how do we begin to comprehend such a concept?

Infinity, by definition, is boundless and limitless, having no beginning or end, no top or bottom, or any other confining factors — because it is always infinitely more than any such limitations. Thus, this is where physics breaks down because it is impossible to measure something that is beyond measurement. A decipherable reality depends upon being measurably less than infinite. So, when I talk about infinity in this book, I am referring to the ultimate origin of the universe that is indecipherable but has the infinite potential to be less than infinite. For the sake of a proper noun, let's call this ultimate origin simply "**the Infinite.**"

Surely, for the Infinite to be less than infinite, it must be relative to its polar opposite of **absolute nothingness**. In other words, the Infinite can only become less than infinite by emerging out of nothing. And this necessitates an intermediate state or a neutral ground that lies somewhere between both sides. This ground state appears to be the universe. It is the energetic process we know as the creation of the cosmos.

No matter how big or small this energetic process may be, and no matter how long it may last, even if it extends into eternity, our universe had a beginning (at the time of the Big Bang), so all things that are part of our universe are **finite**. It is this finite potential that gives the infinite side its less than infinite measurable qualities of space, time, and matter. The infinite side needs to be reducible to such finite definable dimensions that are less than infinite, or it could never be more than nothing.

INFINITE SOURCE

Before the Big Bang, there may have been literally no space and time. But does this really mean there was nothing there at all? I cannot see how it does because there must have been at least the

potential for space and time. So where did this potential come from? Again, we must concede to an infinite regression because if there was a cause of this potential, what was the cause of that cause? Where did that potential come from? The only logical explanation is that it is **potential itself** that is infinite. But what does that really mean?

I think the answer is this: Although it is easy to understand how absolute nothingness is always negatively less than anything and everything, surely we can turn this around to state the total opposite: that is, that the Infinite is always **positively more** than anything and everything. Although just as immaterial as nothing, the infinite side becomes less than infinite by emerging out of the nothingness side. When you think about it, the Infinite could never have been anything tangible because that would limit it. It would be within the confines of space and time, so it would not be infinite (remembering that to be infinite means to be beyond anything measurable). So, all the Infinite can be is infinite in potential.

EMERGENCE

So, for now, let's assume that there is a polar opposite to nothing and that this is infinite, at least in potential. Just as up is contrary to down, the infinite side is contrary to the nothingness side. And this opposition forces a natural middle ground or a compromising medium. This is the universe. It is simply an energetic interrelationship between nothingness and the infiniteness (or the Infinite).

Another way we can look at this interactive process is if we regard infinity as the plus side and nothingness as the minus. Neither side can be anything measurable unless it is in relation to its opposite. That is to say, by adding to nothing, we are taking away from the Infinite. Reverse this, and the Infinite can never be less than infinite unless it is added to the nothingness. So, the infinite plus side, or the **positive** side, becomes less than infinite by becoming positively more than the negative or the minus side. And, of course, it does this by positively emerging out of nothing, thereby revealing the pure potential of the Infinite.

Anything that is more than nothing is part of this unfolding of the Infinite rising up out of the nothingness. Hence, according to this argument, the infinite side is the **first cause** of all existence. But it is the nothingness side that is reducing the infinite side to reveal this **omnipotent** potential. Whatever infinity is, it is forcing whatever nothingness **isn't** into this almighty convergence.

The infinite side has to become more than nothing somehow and the universe is the spectacular result. This means that the universe has an infinite source behind its energetic potential to unfold, and the effect is the astonishing process we witness as the emergence of all creation.

LAWS OF THE UNIVERSE

Just as light contains all potential colors and dark is the absence of color, similarly, the Infinite has all the potential of creation and nothingness is its absence. Everything that exists must have some ultimate cause, and what could be more ultimate than the infinite polar opposite of nothing? Both infinity and nothing are accepted as concepts within science so they must be reconciled. Therefore, I argue that the formation of reality as we know it arises from an interplay between these polar opposite absolutes.

However, although all this interplay is infinite in potential, how it is played out cannot be indiscriminate. The resulting reality must arrange itself into workable patterns, so a highly focused order must become established; otherwise, this convergence between the two sides would be an unfocused blur of indeterminate chaos. And the whole point is to be determinable.

So, rather than just chaotic disorder, the natural attraction is orderliness so that the ultimate source is not limited in its potential to unfold by a lack of workable structure or functional form. In other words, order opens up and stimulates the generative and creative ability of the Infinite. Hence, the universe has configured itself into a creation-stabilizing state. Without this order or the laws and constants of physics, only a futile disorder would follow. But with a workable framework or structure, the unfolding of the universe is not creatively impotent or indeterminable or it is not choked by the narrow potential and unfocused blur of disorder. Instead, the infinite side can forcefully emerge (as the forces of nature) up from the nothingness side.

If there was only one side, or if only the positive direction to infinity existed, what would this side be in relation to? There would be no such thing as nothing. But nothing is something too, if only in the sense of not being anything. It appears that both ultimate extremes can only be anything measurable at all when they are in relation to each other. And the outcome of this relationship is the orderly cosmic theater we call our universe.

RELATIVITY

So, the unfolding potential of the universe is made possible by a naturally occurring orderliness. Because of this orderliness, the infinitely positive side can rise up from the infinitely negative side. And how could there be anything more negative than absolute nothingness (other than perhaps a minus infinity)? But for the infinitely positive side to rise up, there has to be a workable process of some kind, and this we see as the emergent fundamental forces of nature. There would be no "nature" at all if there were nothing for the Infinite to be in relation to. How could this infinitely positive side be anything measurable or tangible or have any properties or dimensions unless it was relative to the nothingness side? This relativity is "nature" itself. By this, I mean it is the natural unfolding of the Infinite. And this infinite side must be a real phenomenon, or all there would be is absolute nothingness.

Think of it like this: if every conceivable thing existed all at once, there would still be the possibility for it all **not to exist** — but in this view, it would be the nothingness that is the potential. Neither infinity nor nothing mean anything unless they are relative to each other in the form of the immense cosmic theater of space and time. As Albert Einstein put it, "The only reason for time is so that everything doesn't happen at once."

12

BIG BANG

According to science, all the energy in the universe and all the matter in its hundreds of billions of galaxies began with the Big Bang. All that we know and understand about nature originated or emerged from whatever caused this Big Bang. Perhaps, before this event, even the concepts of space, time, and matter did not exist (at least, not from the bottom-up perspective or viewpoint).

It was Stephen Hawking who famously pointed out that asking what caused the Big Bang is like asking what is south of the south pole. Just as there is nothing south of the southernmost point of the Earth, there was nothing around before the Big Bang. This analogy is an accepted argument and may be valid, but surely to have a south pole, doesn't there need to be an opposite north pole? If there was nothing for the universe to ascend from, then in my opinion, it must have **descended** from the polar opposite side. From this side, the potential to create space, time, energy, and matter is infinite.

So, although it certainly looks like everything comes from nothing, it is reasonable to state that nothing can come from nothing. In fact, the source origin of our universe, I believe, must be infinitely more than nothing, even if it is nothing measurable. As a thing of potential, this source is the omnipotent power behind, and the *Prime Mover* of, all creation.

Chapter Two

WORKABLE POTENTIAL

In the last chapter, I argued that there is an infinitely positive side behind creation that is the absolute opposite of absolute nothingness. In between these polar opposite sides is the medium we call the universe. Only the infinitely positive side has any potential to unfold, so it is this side that is the source of the **energy** or is the power source that creates everything that has, ultimately, emerged or risen up from absolute nothingness.

Trying to comprehend nothing and infinity can be utterly bewildering. How can there be nothing at all? Not even time and space, or any concept of a medium in which you could put time and space. No light, no temperature, no dimensions or geometry. Just the total absence of anything.

From the opposite perspective, we have the opposite problem. What is infinity? How is it possible that (according to science) the gravitational singularity at the center of a black hole curves space and time infinitely? Or, before the beginning of the universe, how could the *initial singularity* be an infinite state from which all creation has emerged? We can't measure these infinities, either positively toward the Infinite or negatively toward the nothingness, until both sides are in relation to each other. Just as we cannot measure a direction unless it is relative to the opposite direction, or we cannot perceive light unless it is relative to dark, it is through relativity that both sides are measurable. This measurable dimension is the unfolding of space and time, and it is the self-realizing of the Infinite.

POSITIVE VERSUS NEGATIVE

In trying to further conceptualize the relationship between the infinitely positive side and absolute nothingness, let us consider numbers. Of course, numbers go on forever, from number one, two, three, etc., into infinity. But all numbers are relative to zero. Zero is the ground level from which the infinite potential for numbers can emerge. And just as this potential for numbers is relative to zero, the infinite potential for creation is relative to nothing.

By relating the infinite potential behind all creation to the limitless potential of numbers, we can see how you could never reach the end of this potential. The measure of the ultimate source is in its pure potential rather than something measurable. A direction can only be measured relative to the opposite direction. As the opposite direction to the Infinite is toward absolute nothingness, both sides are only measurable when they are in respect of the opposite direction.

Only by the infinitely positive side becoming negatively less than infinite can the negative nothingness side be positively more than nothing. Then, these opposing sides can meet in the middle, and this positive and negative relationship plays out as the pushing and pulling forces of nature. Where else could these fundamental forces come from? Creation is where both sides, or both absolutes, settle into the workable *golden mean* we call the universe. "The Infinite," now reduced to be the positive side behind all positive and negative interactive relationships, can self-arrange into the unfolding cosmos.

ENERGETIC INTERACTIONS OF NATURE

This positive over negative forced relationship is the energetic vitality of the universe. All the liveliness within nature is ultimately down to this self-generating and self-sustaining activity. It is through this process that a universal field of pure potential self-interacts to become particles, which interact to become atoms, molecules, compounds, and so on. Physics evolves into chemistry, which evolves into biology. The whole of nature is built around this evolution of interactivity. Without it, the universe would be dead.

But the universe is not dead; it is vibrantly and energetically alive through all this interactivity. And there must always be energetic activity of some natural order because there will always be the polar opposite of nothing. It is because this opposite of nothing is infinite in its potential to unfold that the potential for creation is infinite. Even if it takes other realms beyond this universe, the capacity to create must be without end.

So, again, the Infinite is unfolding as a medium of interactive potential. Or, as the famous physicist John Wheeler described it, a "self-excited circuit." It is these interactive excitations that self-arrange into workable synergies, which is how the universe and everything in it self-form. The more workably interactive this process becomes, the more expressive nature can become. Life being the most profound part of this cosmic process —

which, I would argue, is how the source of the universe is becoming more thoroughly self-realizable.

Every part of creation is part of this self-expression of the infinite source, which is the positive side of the eternal interactivity between the positive and negative natural forces of nature.

REALIZATION OF PURE POTENTIAL

Let's look at this relationship between the positive and negative sides in terms of *time*.

Time slows down as speed increases (this is *time dilation*, according to Einstein's theory of *special relativity*). Two clocks will display different times if they move through space at different speeds. Imagine if one of the clocks accelerated to reach the speed of light (although, technically, this is impossible because for any object to reach the speed of light, its mass would need to become infinite, which would take infinite energy). Nevertheless, hypothetically speaking, according to the second clock, the first would have slowed to a stop. It seems that time simply doesn't exist beyond the speed of light. But if there is no time, there is no way to unfold the infinite source.

From the perspective of both the positive and negative sides, time is the unfolding of infinite potential that can be measured in terms of time. It is where nothingness becomes more than nothing, and the Infinite becomes less than infinite. And, of course, we see this process working as the unfolding component measures that are time, space, matter, and energy. Without these limiting measures, "the Infinite" is nothing specific or decipherable. Its potential is all-powerful but impotent.

To be realized, the Infinite needs to be realizable. But to be realizable, it must be workable so that the infinite source can continue to unfold. Without settling into a workable state, the ultimate source could not unfold further and so would be limited. But this source is not limited; it is infinite. So, a functional order must self-arrange, and this orderliness is the fundamental laws of physics.

If it were possible to view the universe from the infinite side looking down, we would see this vibrant potential settling into workable patterns. But looking up from the opposite side, these patterns emerge from nothing as the finely tuned laws of the universe. Neither side could be relative to the other without this middle ground (or state) somewhere between absolute nothingness and the absolute infiniteness. So, because the infinite side is forced to deal with how it is more than nothing, it forces this pure potential up out of nothing — this is the infinite potential of the Infinite.

Again, this infinite potential is the "first cause" that powers the forces of nature to create everything from the largest to the tiniest scales. All nature is interactively moving and taking shape by these natural forces. This first cause is literally forcing all creation up out of nothing. From the beginning of the universe to its end, and from tiny fleeting virtual particles to vast ancient galaxies, all things are the consequence of these forces of nature. The theory is that these forces are a forced relationship between the Infinite and the nothingness.

INFINITELY POSITIVE POTENTIAL

Again, assuming that the Infinite is infinitely positive in its potential to be more than nothing, our universe is an outlet for this infinitely positive supply source. According to science, we already understand that the cosmos emerged from the initial singularity — so this must be the infinite source itself that gave rise to the Big Bang.

Just after this Genesis moment at the very beginning of space and time, the preordained laws began to do their work. As mentioned, these laws were so finely adjusted it is almost impossible to put this down to luck, and yet, somehow, this was all worked-out pre-creation. Most scientists admit the huge improbability of this fine-tuning but have difficulty accepting intelligent design because it is simply not scientific to accept the inexplicable. For the fine-tuned conditions to be set as perfectly as they are, there must be an explanation. And if this explanation is that it was all designed by an intelligent designer, then who designed the designer? Science always requires more explanation.

The *Intelligent design* argument is the view that the universe is best explained by an intelligent agent rather than through natural processes or random chance alone. The origins of the intelligent design theory can be traced back to the teleological arguments for the existence of God. This idea has been discussed by philosophers and theologians for millennia. However, today's mainstream scientific consensus is that this intelligent design argument is not widely accepted as a plausible explanation.

So what is accepted? Again, the most popular current theory is that the universe could be just one of many alternate universes. Most of which are not so fine-tuned and, therefore, not so perfectly accommodating for the development of life. In this case, the fine-tuning does not need to have been designed at all, providing it is just one of any number of alternative universes, each with varying laws of physics. If this theory is true, it only strengthens the argument that no matter how we look at it, the ultimate source must be infinite.

But for this infinite source to be anything more than absolutely nothing, it must become something less than infinite. And for this to happen, there must be some form of a self-organizing state. The crucial point is that the whole process is evolving away from the nothingness, so the attraction must always be **toward the Infinite**.

So, how might this natural attraction evolve on a multi-universal (sometimes called the *megaverse*) scale? Could there be an ultimate level or plane of this unfolding potential? Although the potential is infinite, this does not necessarily mean evolution is. Indeed, if there are parallel worlds, it is possible that there is a superlative state or a transcendent realm of celestial balance and harmony.

Chapter Three

A LIVING UNIVERSE

It is simple logic that the universe cannot have been created from nothing without a cause, for the straightforward reason that nothing can come from nothing, let alone the whole cosmos. So, although our universe did not exist before the Big Bang, we cannot say that nothing existed. In fact, according to science, it was an infinite gravitational density (or the initial spacetime singularity) from which the universe emerged. This infinite origin is far from nothing but transcends our understanding of reality. It is where scientific analysis breaks down, yet, it is known that without this infinite source, our universe could not exist.

But does this source have the making to unfold far more than what we can see? If so, what would alternate planes of potential be like? Of course, we cannot know. But we do know that the more expressive the infinite source becomes within our universe, the more it becomes interactively "self-engaged" within itself, or the more it becomes "alive" to itself. Life is the universe at its most alive (at least, that we are aware of), so could there be levels of this aliveness far beyond just this universe?

In the last chapter, I described how the infinitely positive side can only become negatively less than infinite by the negative nothingness side becoming positively more than nothing. It may seem counterintuitive to regard an expanding universe in negative terms, but to emerge from nothing is negative from the perspective of the Infinite. Reverse this, and to reduce the infinite side is positive from the nothingness side. By positively rising from nothing, the Infinite is reduced to deeper and livelier or more absorbed and vividly expressive levels.

In this and the next chapter, I will explain how I believe it is through this expressive potential that all things, including life, emerge. And in the final two chapters, I will delve into what all this could mean in terms of the bigger picture well beyond our limited view of what is possible; and what it also could mean with regard to our own existence, assuming the potential is infinite.

A DEFINITE REALITY

No matter how we may try to define, name, or understand the primary source of creation, we must acknowledge it has infinitely more potential than the nothingness. And although we may have trouble describing this infinite source, we certainly can describe the energy and matter that reside between this source and the nothingness. Just as there is potential for shades between black and white, so there must be the potential for distinction between the infinitely positive side in relation to the infinitely negative side. There must be a channeling of information of some kind, and this channel appears to be, at the very least, our universe.

As already covered, science has revealed that this cosmic channel is so fine-tuned that it is virtually impossible to accept it is due to mere luck. The odds are not one in trillions, but more like one in an unthinkably colossal number (according to the famous physicist Roger Penrose, one part in $10^{10^{123}}$). Any tiny adjustment to the laws would upset the balance enough to make the cosmos (at least as we know it) impossible. Or even cause it to collapse back in on itself or back to nothingness.

So, how did this fine-tuning happen? Again, I believe the answer is that there must be some form of leveling between the Infinite and the absolute nothingness. There has to be a point where both sides can compromise or settle these polar opposite starting points. In some manner, the positive and negative direction of "infinity" must be reconciled. Both sides are fundamental, so this compromising neutral point is also fundamental. This is the ground state that underlies the universe.

Without this focal point for infinite potential, how could there be any specific thing at all? And without fine-tuning, how could there be anything other than indeterminable chaos? Fine-tuning is the opposite of chaos; it is "order," and order is the workable mechanics that are the laws of nature.

Therefore, it looks like it takes order, or it takes the finely tuned laws of the universe for the Infinite to become the working mechanism that is the cosmos. The definiteness of reality needs order because with order comes a functional relationship between the infinitely opposite directions natural to the Infinite. By "directions" I mean the infinite potential **to be** and **not to be**. If infinity is infinite in its potential to be, it is also infinite in its potential not to be. Both directions are conceivable, so there are two directions to the underlying reason why there is anything at all.

You could never reach the end of these polar opposite directions because they are the contrary sides of the same infinitude. Nevertheless, the two sides are complementary in that they are the yin and yang of ancient Eastern philosophy which describes how opposites give rise to each other. You cannot have up without down, soft without hard, hot without cold, etc. But the ultimate opposites are **the Infinite** and **the nothingness.**

Similar to the biblical motif of separating the light from the darkness, the Infinite, as the diametric opposite of nothing, is brought to light by rising out of the absolute nothingness. By "light" here, I am referring to the electromagnetic energy that unfolds the infinitely positive side in relation to the infinitely negative or nothingness side. But because it is the infinitely positive side that is the source of all this unfolding potential, it is this side that is immersed within itself. The effect is that all nature appears as this top-down self-realization of the ultimate source origin that is self-organizing. From galaxies to living cells, all nature is energized by this lively self-organizing process.

IMMATERIAL SOURCE

Science has delved deep into analyzing the physical makeup of the universe, only to find that, at the deepest level, it is not physical at all. According to quantum physics, all particles that make up matter are an indistinct haze of pure potential before settling into definite form. Yet, looking down from the infinite side, this is how the manifestation of matter is bound to appear. This "concentrating down" process engages the infinite side by reducing it or channeling it into measurable resolutions. I submit that this is the *collapse of the wave function* as described in quantum physics (the formation of the actualities of reality through interactive excitations of invisible fields of pure potential).

Perhaps what physicists are observing is the infinite side literally focusing down to become a sharply defined physical reality. To be clear, matter is very real, but as we delve deeper into what it is made of, we see that it emerges from an intangible source of pure potential. From simple elements to the most complex interactively engaged things in the universe, such as intelligent life, everything has risen from this same non-material source that is more fundamental than anything physical. It is the source origin that underlies all creation.

As covered in Chapter One, I believe this underlying non-physical source is the absolute opposite of absolute nothingness. And although this source origin is just as immaterial as the nothingness, it has the infinite capacity to become tangibly less than infinite. Therefore, it is the root cause of everything in existence — from lowly (seemingly) dead matter to highly expressive life. And I imagine humans are an important part of all this unfolding potential.

For most of us, to be alive is to be blinkered from connection to this preeminent source. Like the experience of a virtual reality headset, this concentrated focus creates the illusion we call "the self." But, ultimately, this self is still rooted to its source, the same source as that of all existence, but now in a separated state of *being* and *becoming*.

SENTIENCE

The suffering and competition intrinsic to life seems an unnecessary brutality to the extent that many may ask why there has to be such cruelty in nature. But it is actually essential for the development of life. Without such harsh competition, there would be no need to adapt and therefore no evolution. The fear/comfort and pain/pleasure drives are the basis of evolution. It is the "spiriting up" of sentience.

Without this impetus, or without these impulses that inspirit all living creatures, life would be totally unmoved and indifferent. In other words, the ability of life to interact would not be so focused; it would be less self-aware or even oblivious to any distinction between pain and pleasure, good and bad, penalty or reward. Essentially, it would be non-sentient matter. Although non-sentient matter is essential as it is the infrastructure for all nature, the whole point of creation is in the unfolding of the Infinite, which has infinite creative potential. And because this potential is infinite, why would this process stop at shallow, meaningless, inanimate matter with little expressive potential?

The only reason energy exists at all, in my opinion, is to force the potential of the infinite side up out of the nothingness side. And because the infinite side has infinite potential, it is logical that it will become increasingly immersed within itself — self-organizing into complex formations or more and more engaged or concentrated patterns of potential. And the most complex pattern of unfolding potential that we know of is life. However, the more life becomes concentrated on its narrow but essential needs to survive and thrive, the more it appears separated from the source of its true being. This source is still the same source as that of all creation, but now focused down to self-organizing, **self-realizing**, deeply involved levels.

In theory, there is nothing to stop life from being common and spreading all over the universe. If this is the case, then looking at creation as a whole throughout all space and time, and for many billions or trillions of years into the future, it is difficult to imagine that the universe is dead. In fact, on the contrary, it is particularly through life that the universe is vibrantly alive through the evolution of this interactive potential.

Current scientific thinking suggests that many billions of potentially life-hosting planets exist in the Milky Way galaxy alone. Add to this an estimated one hundred billion galaxies within the observable universe, and if there are also any number of alternative universes, then the mind boggles at how much potential there could be for life. But because all this potential has emerged from the same ultimate source, all things are unified by this source. Therefore, we cannot begin to imagine the true potential of this unification in terms of a much bigger picture.

So, what is the significance of consciousness as part of this whole process? I will cover this topic next, along with why I believe there is no reason to dismiss the notion that higher realms of consciousness exist. In fact, not only do they exist, but probably have links to this realm. All things stem from the same ultimate source, after all.

Chapter Four

WHAT IS AWARENESS?

In the last chapter, I reasoned that the infinite source behind the universe is self-realizing. In this chapter, I will endeavor to delve deeper and argue how this self-realization is the beginning of, or root origin of the evolution of **awareness**.

Remember, the Infinite can only be less than infinite by emerging from nothing. Before this, both sides are absolutely or perfectly stable and constant. Only a forced intermediary excitement causes so much destabilization. By *intermediary excitement*, I mean an energetically lively condition was forced to form between the two polar opposite sides, which stirs up the cosmic energy that creates the whole physical universe.

But does this mean that the cosmos is lively but not alive? If all nature is the result of this same process, or is created from the same cosmic energy, why is it that only some of this nature is considered alive? How do living things differ from non-living things? The answer, I believe, and as inferred in the last chapter, is that life is simply the more interactively concentrated parts of a living universe.

EVOLUTION

Everything that exists from the Big Bang onward has emerged as part of the unfolding of the infinitely positive source. Patterns of complexity are how this source is becoming increasingly immersed or self-interactively engaged — and this is how the source is awakening to its own infinite potential by self-realizing to more and more concentrated levels. By *concentrated*, I mean "focusing in" on interactive potential. The more concentrated this evolution becomes, the more the universe becomes alive to itself. And this shows up in the most lively way that we know — **life itself.**

Beyond its basic function of reproduction, life requires discernment to navigate the challenge of being alive, i.e., interacting and surviving within an environment. This highly involved evolution requires self-managing capabilities, no matter how simple, evolving to the levels we know as perception, attention, and alertness. These are the interactive faculties necessary for life to endure and adapt, which is the nature of being alive. In other words, **awareness**.

AWARENESS IS TOP-DOWN

Nothing can be created that is beyond or outside of the infinite source, so in this respect, all creation is top-down or is inwardly focused. This is how the source differentiates itself from nothing. From the nothingness side looking up, the universe is not in any way self-realizing because it is emerging from nothing. But, again, from the opposite side looking down, creation is self-unfolding. For an analogy, let's again turn to numbers.

Imagine trying to count to infinity. Obviously, you can't because no matter what number you reach, there will always be higher numbers. This fact shows how, when considering the concept of infinity, we cannot infer it as anything specific or measurable. However, by defining a specific number, we can see that infinity is reducible when it needs to be finitely expressible. And, similar to the expressible potential of numbers, any point in space and time reduces infinite potential to an actual potential. Everything in existence is part of this top-down process of becoming less than infinite. But, again, there is another property natural to this top-down process, and that is the evolution of *awareness*.

It seems logical that awareness evolves from the same ultimate origin as the rest of nature. The more the self-realizing infinite source unfolds within itself, the more it is alive to itself. From simple but still self-interacting elements to the highly evolved complex entities we call **life**, there is a wide variety of this aliveness and, therefore, awareness.

INTERACTIVE FORCES OF NATURE

Remember that the infinite origin of the universe is not anything physical as that would be limiting. However, it is infinite in two directions: positively and negatively. The negative side is infinite in the direction of absolute nothingness, while the positive side is infinite toward the ultimate source. The universe mediates between both sides, so it is in a perpetual state of positive and negative interactivity — which we see as the pushing and pulling forces of nature. These forces push to create quantum waves, the positive aspects of the fundamental forces, and dark energy. The pulling forces create gravity, the negative element of the fundamental forces, and dark matter. The universe is made up of these natural positive and negative interactive forces. However, only the positive side of this process is unfolding, so all existence is an expressiveness of this positive side in relation to the negative side.

But how does awareness fit in? The answer makes more sense when we look at nature top-down rather than bottom-up as typically viewed by science. Of course, there is no self-awareness at lower levels of physical reality (atomic, molecular, chemical, etc.), but this is still the beginning of the evolution of self-interactivity. It is all part of the awakening of the infinite source. Therefore, life as we know it is an evolved form of self-interactivity emerging from simpler forms. But it is not matter that is evolving into life; it is an alive universe evolving **AS matter**. In other words, our body is not aware of itself, the universe is aware AS the body, or as part of a living universe.

Of course, this metaphysical argument cannot be empirically proven because science struggles to even understand what conscious awareness is. This is because science measures bottom-up **objective** facts such as physical matter. I believe consciousness is a top-down **subjective** phenomenon, so it is far more difficult to prove scientifically. But, again, I submit that it is all part of how the infinite source is self-realizing in relation to absolute nothingness.

WHAT IS MEMORY?

The infinite side can only be more than the nothingness side by emerging bottom-up out of nothing. Of course, at the same time, it is immersed within itself or is internally or inwardly engaged, which is how all creation is self-processed.

But another term for this processability is **memory**. Without memory, how could any form of interactivity be possible? The evolution of memory and awareness are two aspects of the same information-gathering nature of creation. Although a computer is not in any way self-aware, it can only function by having a working memory, and all reality is the product of the memory of information; beginning with the laws of physics. How could the universe's natural laws be carried out if they were not remembered? However, unlike a computer, the universe is not an artificial machine but more like a living organism, or is more mindlike than physical. I am far from the first to suggest that the deepest level of reality functions like a **universal mind**.

Again, it is not matter evolving to create awareness, it is awareness evolving **as** or **through** matter. From this perspective, awareness **IS** the universe or contains it, rather than the universe containing awareness — which is why the cosmos is more like a living organism than a machine. Hence, so are its naturally evolving offspring. **Life** is the inspirited progeny of an alive universe. And because of life, the infinite source has far more potential to evolve subjectively. Pursue the evolution of this subjective aliveness, and what emerges is an intelligent **self-awareness**.

SELF-AWARENESS

In trying to interpret further and describe awareness, let's approach it from a different angle. Assuming that the universe did emerge from an infinitely dense source (the *initial singularity*), we must then ask, infinite compared to what? The answer must be compared to its polar opposite, which is infinite nothingness. And this polar opposite must naturally resist it since it is contrary to it. What else could cause such a reaction as the Big Bang and all that has developed after this event? It would be far easier just to be nothing and do nothing. But that would mean not being infinitely greater than nothing. So, something had to give. Hence, all creation.

So, even before our universe got started, there must have always been the potential to differentiate between these polar opposite sides. Perhaps nothing had ever been created before the start of this universe (which I doubt), but the potential for it to unfold must have always been a very real prospect waiting to happen.

However, if the source of the universe is infinite, why doesn't everything happen? Why are there infinite possibilities that will never be realized, or why are the forces of nature limiting the infinite source to finite expressions? But to be everything means to be nothing **specific**. Without some form of finite self-organization, the source can only remain non-physical and therefore in a non-creative state. But this defeats the object of becoming more than nothing, so some bounded structure or limiting form must be fostered in order to continue to unfold. Consequently, there is the necessity for time, space, and energy, or energetic effects. Without this self-organization, the universe could only regress into stagnation. But this stagnation is limiting, and the ultimate source cannot be limited, so it must be reduced to such structure or form that is conducive to continuing to unfold or evolve.

Therefore, the infinite side pushes up out of the nothingness side but requires a self-organizing process to do so, which explains why nature also abhors a vacuum. The universe is a self-organizing system, and it is the opposite of dead. In fact, it is the quintessence of *alive*. And the pinnacle of this aliveness is awareness. Again, this awareness then evolves to deeply integrated or complexly involved levels. And the most complexly integrated thing in the universe (that we are aware of) is the human brain — which, of course, is not only the controlling and coordinating center of the nervous system but is the seat of thought. Thinking is part of awareness, but on a deeper level than thinking is the observer of the thinking, or that deep subjective element that is aware of thoughts. This, I believe, is the source of the universe reduced to fragments. Separated (at least for a while) simply because it takes a focused discernment for a complexly integrated awareness.

Awareness, then, appears to be an intrinsic and integral part of the unfolding self-realization of the universe. This deeply engaged process is still the natural evolution of the infinite source — but honed in as a concentrated awareness and the illusion of being separate. Like everything else that is part of the unfolding of reality, individual awareness, or consciousness, is part of the self-realizing of the ultimate source.

BEING ALIVE IS ALL IN THE MIND

Every expressive potential to create reality must lie somewhere between the potential for nothing and the infinite potential for everything. But because of these two polar opposite aspects, there are two perspectives: bottom-up and top-down. It is easy to understand how, from the bottom up, there is no capacity for self-aware mindfulness — because we are coming from the starting point of absolutely nothing. But what about the other way around?

Just as you could not go further north when at the north pole, the Infinite cannot be more than infinite. Therefore, all it can do is self-realize and self-express. This infinite side is perfectly stable before all this energetic work, just as the absolute nothingness is also perfectly stable. Both sides are absolute, so they are unchanging. But an intermediating level is bestirred or roused into existence by intervening and destabilizing both sides. There could be higher and lower states (known as parallel universes or alternate dimensions), and there probably are, but our universe is the only one we are sure of.

So, our vibrant universe is the product of a necessity for the infinite source to foment its potential to be more than nothing. This potential is forced to assert itself somehow, and universal energy is this work in progress. It is the Infinite concentrated down to high resolutions or settling into conceivable potentials (this, as mentioned in the last chapter, is the collapse of the wave function in accordance with the fundamental principles of quantum mechanics).

Just as our mind has the potential to generate any thought but requires focus to do so, the source of all creation also needs to be brought into focus. This focusing of the infinite side is what conceives the universe. The universe's ability to facilitate this process of **focusing** is what allows anything to become distinct from everything else. All creation is a manifestation of this universal mind-like focusing-in, or focusing down, from the infinite side.

Again, this infinite side can only be less than infinite, it cannot be more, so it can only self-realize. All interactivity within nature stems from this self-realization of the Infinite. Our own personal mind and awareness is also part of this universal self-realizing process, so this is the deepest nature of our evolving consciousness. Non-living matter, such as a rock, is simply an inanimate part of the stage setting. Though involved in the show, lifeless elements are not animatedly complex, so there is no need for the interactively responsive feedback that is awareness. At least, not to the level of a spirited self-awareness.

LIFE FORCE

So, everything that is a part of the universe is a definable part of the infinite source. Otherwise, it would still only be the unfocused blur of infinitely unrealized potential. This definability is what we call reality. To be alive is to be a particularly concentrated part of this reality. In essence, the self-perception of life is part of the self-realization of the infinite source. The more this self-perception develops as a personal mind, the more it appears detached from the universal mind by this selfhood.

If you are still confused by what I mean by a *universal mind*, consider this: In chapter one, I described why I believe the ultimate source of the universe (as the opposite of nothing) is infinite. This infinite side is just as immaterial as nothing, but with infinitely more potential to evolve up out of the nothingness side. Again, the infinite side could never have been anything tangible before creation because that would give it a definition that is limiting and, therefore, not infinite. Consequently, everything in existence is rooted to this intangible infinite side that is "focusing in" on potentials in a conceiving mindlike way. This is my definition of the universal mind.

Our own mind may be a personal domain, but it is still a part of the universal mind that is the ultimate source of all things, including all awareness, and it is the **life force** that breathes life into the physical body.

Another way to describe how the universal mind is reduced to this life force, or the intangible element that keeps us alive, is if we regard life as the micro mindfulness of a macro mind. The universal mind is the macro mind that is the infinite source awakening to its own infinite potential. Whereas micro minds are concentrated constituents of the macro mind. The more engaged or channeled the macro mind, the more it is reduced to a micro mind, distinct from the whole by this concentration.

Therefore, I submit that the ultimate source, however it is envisioned, is all-involved, similar to how a computer is in running its software. The more interactively engaged this source is, the more it channels into the micro minds we call life. This, I believe, is why there are practices in mindful meditation that enable people to feel they can connect to deeper levels of the mind. Such meditative states let go of the ego (a construct created by the mind) by merging with the universal consciousness that connects us all. Indeed, meditation techniques have been practiced for thousands of years throughout the world, backing up the argument that deeper regions of the mind are part of this universal mind — and implying that this universal or macro mind underlies all existence and is the precursor to individual minds. I believe all minds are part of how the infinite source is self-realizing to concentrated levels of awareness that we know as the sensibilities of life (described in philosophy as *qualia*) and, of course, to the level we know as human consciousness and the life force.

Therefore, the evolution of consciousness is as much a part of the unfolding of the infinite source as anything else. But we are forced to wonder, what then is the outlook or what are the prospects for this evolution of consciousness? Especially when we consider that infinite potential cannot be limited, otherwise, it would not be infinite. I will provide further thoughts on this later in the book.

CONCENTRATED POTENTIAL

Irrespective of the physical level of what it means to be alive, and in this I include the mental functioning of the brain, or the brain's level of mind. At the deeper levels of the mind, it appears we merge with the non-tangible source of all creation. This is the life force level of our being.

Just as energy is more fundamental than matter (matter needs energy, but energy doesn't need matter), so this life force is more fundamental than the body. The surface ego level of the mind is a fleeting thing in any case, going through many phases throughout its short existence. But this transience cannot be all there is to the mind, in which case, it seems to me that this ego level is not the whole of us but an impression upon the whole — or upon that part of us that runs infinitely deeper.

All forms of existence, whether physical or mental, are integral to the self-realizing of the infinite source. Again, this self-realization allows the Infinite to distinguish itself from the nothingness. Just as you cannot project darkness because dark is only the absence of light, so absolute nothingness is only the absence of the Infinite.

Therefore, two fundamental aspects underlie all reality: one is perpetually adding to nothing, while the other is subtracting from the opposite side. One side is objective, the other subjective. One side is awakening, the other witnessing. Just as light is only definable relative to darkness, the Infinite is only definable relative to the nothingness. Hence, the Infinite is self-defining relative to this nothingness, with the potential for this process to evolve to increasingly complex or intricately profound levels. But what can any of this energetic activity be if it is not the infinite source interacting within itself? It is what connects all things so that this source can know itself as less than infinite. And it is through intricate complexity that the source becomes more thoroughly self-known. This is **omniscience**. At sensitive and intimately engaged levels, a deep self-knowingness can reveal itself — indicating the true significance and value of life.

In having the potential to become, it seems the source of creation has the potential to behold. And no doubt at the forefront of this self-beholding aspect intrinsic to nature is the highly evolved self-awareness we know as human consciousness.

Chapter Five

HOW THERE IS PURPOSE

Even if space and time continue forever, this does not mean they are infinite since there was a starting point with the Big Bang 13.8 billion years ago. For the universe to be truly infinite, it cannot have had a beginning.

Remember, the first cause of the universe is the absolute opposite of absolute nothingness. Only an infinitely forcible resistance to this nothingness could cause the forces of nature to spring up from nothing. And according to science, the universe did in fact arise from just such an infinite cause, labeled the initial singularity (which contained all the energy and spacetime of the universe).

For the infinite side to affect the nothingness side, the nothingness side must affect the infinite side. **Involution** of the Infinite is **evolution** to the nothingness. Hence, the evolution of the universe from nothing. One side is the infinite source with no beginning, the other is the unfolding of this source with no end. And again, this is the yin and yang of Chinese philosophy (as mentioned in chapter three). Yin is the negative side, yang the positive. There can be no positive without negative, no give without take, no bright without dark, no male without female, etc. Natural complementary interactions are the harmony of the universe by converging to create and influence everything within it.

OMEGA POINT

The positive side is the infinite side, or the infinite potential to be more than the negative nothingness. This unfolding potential channels into the forces of nature that we see working as dynamically charged *energy*. This energy then creates everything from nothing, and the infinite side, or **source**, can evolve toward wherever infinite potential may lead. And this infinite source cannot be limited in what it has the potential to create so long as it is a functioning reality of some form or other. It is infinite, after all. So there must literally be infinite possibilities. But could there be a limit to evolution? This is an interesting question.

Perhaps only equilibrium is the limiting factor or the so-called *Omega Point*; this is a supposed future state when everything spirals toward unification. The term was coined by French Jesuit priest, scientist, and philosopher, *Pierre Teilhard de Chardin*. It is the spiritual belief that the universe is evolving toward a higher level of material complexity and consciousness. Maybe the attraction of equilibrium is how the eternal pushing and pulling forces of nature will ultimately evolve, or resolve, this unfolding celestial potential.

As covered, it is also feasible that the source of our universe can create alternate planes of existence. The true potential may be impossible for us to comprehend, but if the source really is infinite, this potential to unfold must also be infinite. And if this potential can branch out to other planes of existence (and according to theoretical physics, this is possible), then there is nothing to stop this creation process from creating on a scale far beyond what we can currently observe.

ALL THINGS ARE ONE

If the universe could tell us where it came from, I think the answer would be, "I am of the Infinite." Meaning, the infinitely positive side behind nature. And asking any part of the universe, no matter how infinitesimally small, would be the same as asking the universe as a whole. By this I mean that if we could ask any tiny part of the cosmos, even to *Planck scales* (the smallest possible size), we would receive the same feedback as asking the whole. From the smallest to the largest scale, and within all space and time from its beginning to its end, the unfolding of all creation is a mediation between the positive and negative potential directions of infinity. Without this compromise, there could be no distinction between either side.

This mediation is the neutral ground that differentiates between what can and can't exist, or what is in tune and out of tune with the potentials for creation. The whole of nature as we know it is at least part of this process that is unfolding as space and time and as an expanding universe. And it is because the universe is expanding that many people may naturally wonder what it is expanding into. It cannot be space and time because the universe **is** space and time (or spacetime). The answer appears to be that it is expanding into absolutely nothing. If there is a boundary to this universe, it is also the boundary of space and time.

By being pulled down from the infinite side, all creation is pushed up out of the nothingness side. But before settling to become this high-resolution reality, the universe is a field of pure unsettled or irresolute energetic potential that is vibrating or fluctuating or oscillating between both sides. At the point of convergence, this positive and negative wavering is resolved with a particular resonance (or frequency of vibration) that forms the reality we see unfolding as energy and matter.

Take any part of this energy and matter at any given moment within the space and time; by this, I mean anything in the entire universe that has ever been or ever will be. Zoom in closer and closer, deeper and deeper into what it is made of, and eventually, it disappears (at smaller than Planck scales) into the infinite source that the whole universe materialized from in the first place.

Any theory that tries to explain what is happening at this unimaginably small scale (such as *Loop Quantum Gravity* and *String Theory*) still requires the intangible infinite source from which the cosmos emerged. Hence, we could keep delving deeper and deeper forever without reaching a level at which reality begins. And more obviously, if we pull away, we could keep retracting forever (even at the speed of light) without ever reaching a point where it no longer exists. However, none of this matters because only the original point of focus where we began is where infinity both starts and ends. Everything before, after, within, or all around this point of focus is infinite or is the infinite potential that created this expressive reality in the first place.

Therefore, if the whole universe is *of the Infinite*, any infinitesimal point, component, or portion of the universe is *of the Infinite*, too. The first cause of all reality, as reasoned by Spinoza, is both the Creator and the created. It is the source of the whole and any part of that whole. All things are one.

FROM THE ABSTRACT TO THE ACTUAL

So, if all things are created from the same single infinite source that transcends the universe, what is the point or purpose of all this work to become less than infinite?

Again, I believe the answer is in the fact that there are naturally opposite directions to infinity. To infinitely extend in one direction is only possible relative to the opposite direction. And it is this relativity that quantifies both sides. It is how the positive side is reduced to this energetic process of becoming more than the negative nothingness side.

Only through this natural attraction to be quantifiable and determinable can the abstract potential of the infinite potential become an actual workable potential. This is why all nature self-arranges into the functioning system and synergies that is the creation of matter. And this is why the universe is so astonishingly fine-tuned.

It is possible that it could take evolution on a multi-universal scale for this fine-tuning to be worked out. But whether this is true or not, the laws of our universe have been very precisely set somehow. And, as I have argued, this is at least one way in which the infinite source can be reduced to forms of reality that are less than infinite. The stage is set for the sharply focused unfolding of the pure potential of the infinite source.

ENTROPY

But what, some will rightly argue, about the second law of thermodynamics, or entropy? This is the fundamental law of the universe that tends toward the opposite direction. That is, instead of moving toward the ordered realization, or the development of the potential of the universe, entropy is ultimately causing it to decline into disorder. Some scientists reason that entropy will eventually (after an extraordinarily long time) cause the universe to return to nothing or perhaps to the singularity from which it emerged. But whatever the outcome, before then, an unimaginable amount of creation will have the potential to play out because of the attraction forces that create matter and structure within the universe (the exact opposite of the disorder caused by entropy). But why does there have to be any degeneration at all?

Remember, two absolutes are underlying and overlaying all nature: the infinite plus side and the infinite minus or the nothingness side, and both fundamental sides naturally yield to each other. This yield cultivates space, time, and the physical matter that is necessary for there to be a **frame of reference**. To have a frame of reference is to be definable to some measure or some degree as space and time. Only the infinite positive and negative absolutes can have no degree of measure, such as no beginning or end. But the universe must have a finite frame of reference so it cannot last for all eternity, and an eventual end is part of the course. However, this course must also be part of an eternally bigger picture. Who knows what all this may mean in terms of this bigger picture, but it is probably far more positive than we can imagine, as I'll cover in the next chapter on *transcendence*.

ILLIMITABLE POTENTIAL

As science tries to understand the workings of the immense expanse of the cosmos, and analyzes nature to deeper and deeper depths in its structure and makeup, we can only marvel at what is revealed. From grand clusters of ancient galaxies to the tiniest of particles, we are seeing how the source of the universe is unraveling its infinite potential to create. We cannot assume that there is a limit to this creative potential because to do so is to suggest that the source of it all is less than infinite, and so could run out of potential. It does look (because of entropy) as if it is possible that creation could fizzle out, in which case its source is not infinite. But looking at the bigger picture beyond this universe, this source can never be exhausted because if it has the potential to create but only to a limited degree, then it is not the absolute opposite of absolute nothingness. As covered in chapter one, if the nothingness side is infinitely negative, then the infinite side is infinitely positive. And if it is infinite, it can never be nothing.

Of course, again, there is a middle ground (the universe), which is how the infinitely positive side is unfolding its infinite potential. But this does not necessarily mean the universe is infinite, only that its source is. Moreover, if this source is infinite, then it must have the potential for infinite possibilities — but these have to be worked out as workable possibilities, or as the interactive facts of reality that create information. And, for the reasons covered in the last chapter, I believe the memory of information is preserved forever. This memory is not stored in atoms or molecules, or even brains; I maintain that it is part of the self-realizing of the ultimate source of all creation. All the information unfolding down from this infinite source requires memory just as much as memory requires information.

So, if the source of the universe has a perfect memory for its own unfolding potential, we must wonder what all this self-realizing information means on a larger scale. Surely this memory is not constrained or disconnected by separate or alternate realities or higher dimensions. After all, there is only one source; the same source that is behind all levels of potential.

COSMOLOGICAL NATURAL SELECTION

A theory that I think supports the arguments outlined in this chapter is the *cosmological natural selection* hypothesis, as proposed by theoretical physicist Lee Smolin, along with the contributions of Bryce DeWitt and John Archibald Wheeler. And this theory, as I understand it, is based on the concept of natural cosmic evolution. Just like anything else that is alive, universes grow, die, and reproduce.

According to this theory, the other side of the infinite density of a black hole is a *white hole*. And because a white hole is a black hole in reverse, instead of pulling space and time into a singularity, it pushes it out. Thus, it follows that our Big Bang could have been a white hole or the opposite side of the black hole of another universe.

The premise is that the more black holes a universe can create, the more white holes are created (alternate universes). And the healthier a universe is in terms of its physical constants and finely tuned laws, the more likely this is to happen. Even slight differences in the fundamental constants will mean some universes work out better than others, but it takes optimal conditions for a stable universe of black holes to form. These, naturally, are the ones that survive long enough to create more black holes. Any mutations found not to be optimal, for instance, with unworkable or fruitless constants, would not be stable enough, or would not survive long enough to create black holes themselves and so would not pass on their properties through offspring or descendent white holes.

To fully realize the significance of this process, consider how, over eons, the most successful universes would be the ones passing on their cosmic information this way. Through this **evolution**, better and better patterns of creation could develop on a multiverse scale. Could this be the reason that our universe was so finely tuned from its inception? Other than a Supreme Being, or God, where else could this intelligent design have come from?

The point to bear in mind regarding this scientifically respectable theory is that the better a universe is at making black holes, the better it is at passing on its properties to other universes that are making stars and planets. Therefore, the better it is at making life. And the better it is at making life, the better it is at enabling the *Infinite Source* to self-realize, become alive to itself, and awaken to its own infinite potential.

ASCENSION OF CONSCIOUSNESS

From all this, we see that evolution could be operating on a scale far grander than we can observe. But it is the complexly concentrated levels of **life** that unfold the most profound potentials of creation. It seems sensible to assume that the ever-unfolding infinite source requires the creation of ever more involved interactive complexity in order to become truly self-known.

I see it like this: The more deeply immersed the Infinite becomes in its unfolding potential, the more this celestial potential is focused to complex levels of matter. Matter then evolves to the self-awareness levels of life. And as already covered, these are the micro minds as part of a macro universal mind. Of course, we are now talking in terms of the **spiritual**: the infinite source concentrated to sensitive levels by this evolving awareness.

This spiritual element is the developing soul, or the self-realizing aspect (or the life force) that is mediating between body and source. Hence, the soul is a part of the top-down realization of the infinite source itself. Logically speaking, and assuming there are multi-dimensional potentials for this realization, this spiritual element must be able to transition, or passage (pass over), or progress from one state of reality to another. And the phenomenon of spiritual growth suggests that the soul is in preparation for these higher planes of existence (*spiritual transcendence*).

Before we dismiss such notions, we must recognize how much there is that we do not yet understand. Is there anything beyond our universe? Are singularities connections to other dimensions, or parallel universes? Einstein's theory of relativity allows for such gateways to other realities.

So, although it may be impossible for anything physical to move on to these alternative realms, what about those elements just as much a part of reality but not physical, such as the emergence of mind, soul, intelligence, love? No doubt these meaningful values will make a greater impression on the unfolding bigger picture than mere physical qualities, and so will have more significance as part of higher potentials for existence.

It is therefore possible, in fact, I would say it is highly probable, that spiritual consciousness, or **the soul**, has the potential to transition as naturally as there are evolving levels of creation. Remember, the positive potential of the ultimate source is infinite, so it is feasible to assume there must be far more positive potential for existence than just our layer of reality. Science recognizes the possibility of multiple dimensions or alternative planes of potential, so there could well be alternative planes of being having connections or links to this layer through the multiversal memory of information.

Therefore, assuming that there is such a process as "transmigration of the soul" (or *metempsychosis*, as believed in ancient philosophies worldwide), then perhaps there is a continuum of consciousness so advanced as to be the fruition of all levels of the evolution of spiritual potential (the omega point). If so, we could not even imagine how advanced the ascension of consciousness might be or become.

Of course, all this is in no way provable, but it is far more plausible to my mind than the notion that there is no meaning to life, or no lasting significance to the unfolding of all creation. If there are multiple universes, as proposed by many scientists, then there is a good chance that a soul is part of this multi-level reality. Indeed, it would seem logical. If the ultimate source is infinite in its potential to create, why would it do anything less?

Chapter Six

TRANSCENDENCE

Some materialist scientists ardently claim that there is no deeper meaning behind the universe than what is created and developed by the physical substance we can observe — inferring that it is all just a lucky accident or a fluke happening. This view has filtered down into much of society, leaving many people deducing that, if this is true, it means there is no deeper meaning to their own existence either.

But to assert these uninspiring ideas is only opinion based on conjecture or interpretation. Although vindicated by observational data such as in physics and cosmology, this disheartening logic is only in respect of analyzing what can be observed, not what is possible. In this book, I hope I have persuaded you that the source of all reality has the potential to create far more than what we can observe. And it is through **life** that this source is self-realizing to more deeply focused and, therefore, more meaningful levels of unfolding potential.

The more concentrated this unfolding potential becomes (or evolves), the more it appears to require some form of high-resolution feedback as part of the process. It is living consciousness that is graced with this calling. And if the potential of consciousness is also infinite, I don't think we can even imagine what this might mean in terms of a higher purpose.

EQUANIMITY

To reiterate my argument: If the ultimate source is infinite, it must have infinite potential to be more than nothing. That is to say, the source must be infinitely evolving away from the nothingness. This infiniteness cannot be physical in its purest state, as that would be a limited state. So it must be a nonmaterial state, honing in on how it can be less than infinite. And if this potential is infinite, the significance is infinite.

As I say, some scientists insist that there can be no lasting meaning to the universe, therefore, no lasting purpose to life. Dismissing any possibility of an eternal spiritual element, and that we should come to terms with this fact. Some even suggest we should welcome it because to no longer exist is less scary than existing forever. The argument goes that it is not death that is frightening, but eternity. I can see the logic of that reasoning, but to my mind, it depends on your understanding of "existing for all eternity." If it means spiritual transcendence toward harmony and equilibrium, or *equanimity*, rather than living for all eternity among the same disharmonies and evils, these are very different outlooks.

According to the ancient teachings of Buddhism, equanimity is the realization of a state of balance and harmony that leads to wisdom, truth, compassion, and love without hostility. I understand anyone who might wish to challenge such traditional beliefs, particularly in light of the advancements in science. But to claim there is no purpose or deeper meaning to our existence is just an opinion that cannot be proven scientifically. Therefore, suggesting pointlessness in the name of science seems unnecessary and unwise.

Understandably, throughout the ages, people of the world have supposed creation to be by the will of a personal deity, or God. Personally, I imagine the ultimate reason to be an infinite mind-like source rather than a supernatural (anthropomorphic) being. But if this universal mind can take form at a level beyond our understanding, then I can see the reasoning behind this argument. Whatever the truth, I think we must come to terms with the fact that science cannot tell us what this ultimate first cause is, so I do not believe we should turn to science to answer this most important of questions.

THE MAKE-UP OF ALL CREATION

With all this said, we cannot overstate just how much science has positively impacted our modern world. In fact, we can only marvel at its findings and paradigms. *String theory*, for example, might well explain the deepest level of reality. The so-called *strings* are tiny massless vibrations, so small that we cannot observe them directly, only their consequence. But, according to this theory, these vibrations are the most fundamental constituent of everything that exists.

The rate at which something vibrates is referred to as its **frequency**, and everything in the universe vibrates at a unique frequency or has a particular resonance that differentiates it from everything else. Whether it is physical and factual or mental and emotional, this channeling of frequencies down from the infinite side is how they emerge up and out of the nothingness side.

It seems to me that the makeup of all creation is based on this "tuning in" of frequencies, or energetic wavelengths of potential. Apparently, string theory also requires extra dimensions of space and time and multiple parallel universes, so who knows what all this means in terms of otherworldly potential, or how it all fits in terms of the self-realization of the ultimate source.

HIGHER MODELS OF REALITY

If the infinite source is **forced** to be less than infinite, and the nothingness is **forced** to become more than nothing, no wonder there are **forces** of nature. These forces must come from somewhere and must be forcing something to happen. This "something," at the very least, is our universe self-arranging into patterns of natural order. As we know, this natural order involves highly expressive interactions or evolving complexity. But, because the Infinite is limitless in this potential to create, the potential for more and more creative complexity must also be limitless. Life is proof of the astonishing potential of this complexity, but the attraction is always toward frictionless harmony, stability, symmetry, and order. And this attraction is universal.

From the stable orbit of planets around stars to the homeostasis in every cell of the body, constancy and balance will always be the optimal condition or state that the source of the universe will be attracted to create. Again, we can only guess what this means in terms of multiple universes, extra dimensions, or the advancement of pure potential, both physical and non-physical. Nevertheless, sooner or later, and no matter how much upheaval is involved in becoming more than nothing, the draw is always to settle into equilibrium — but not without first unfolding a lot of information about what works and what doesn't. And because the unfolding of information is always remembered (as covered in chapter four), I believe the processing of all this potential must have an impact, or create an impression on higher planes of potential. In other words, it is conceivable that this world has some significance to the next, or to further models of reality and higher potentials for existence.

WHAT IS TIME?

Before it is reduced to rise out of nothing, as already said, the Infinite is stable. This must be the case since there is nothing to destabilize it other than its own potential to be less than infinite — and it is this infinite "potential" that underlays all reality. Just as you cannot have uphill unless it is relative to downhill, so you cannot have the Infinite unless it is relative to the nothingness. Otherwise, what is it in relation to? Infinite compared to what? As natural opposites, the infinite side contends with the nothingness side, which is why it has the potential to become less than infinite.

From the creation of stellar nurseries forming stars to the tiniest of particles, the infinite side is the infinite source unfolding everything that exists. But before it is reduced to become all creation, this infinite source is utterly positive in its potential to become less than infinite. It must be infinitely positive, or else it would be less than infinite. In Hinduism, this infinite positive stability is considered the ultimate unchanging reality, or the highest principle. In science, it is the ground state of zero entropy before the Big Bang. But however it is described, anything that deviates away from this infinite stability is negative, anything that moves toward it is positive. Time can only go in one direction because it is there for only one reason: to unfold the infinite source. But in order for the source to be negatively less than infinite, it must, through time, become positively more than nothing.

POTENTIAL REALMS OF EXISTENCE

Suppose for a moment that you had never lived, therefore, you have never had experience of how you fit in as part of the unfolding of the Infinite. You would have no idea or concept of what it means to experience, or of what you are capable of being or becoming. You would be nothing.

But, just as nature abhors a vacuum, for the same reason, the infinite source of nature abhors nothingness. So, you are not nothing, you are part of creation. Therefore, you are part of the unfolding of the source of creation. And because the source is eternal, the potential for existence must also be eternal. Indeed, it is almost impossible to deny the possibility that there is far more potential for existence than we can detect, or that is going on beyond our field of view. So, can we believe in an afterlife? I think that we can and should. But where could such realms of existence reside?

Well, as already said, theoretical physicists already talk in terms of multiple realities and alternate dimensions, so it is not beyond reason that there are other realms for existence. This makes sense because the source of the universe is infinite, so it **must** create more than we can see. Whether we accept it is possible to transcend to these alternative planes of being depends on whether we accept it is all part of the realization of the **same ultimate source**. And, if it is, then why would just one plane of existence be all there is?

If information is never lost (fact of physics), why would the impression of a soul be lost forever? As described in chapter five, the emergent value of a soul (including the mind, love, and spirit) will leave impressions on the source because these are positive values as part of this infinitely positive source. This source is self-realizing relative to nothingness, so positive values are always in the right direction.

It seems to me that all things that exist are part of this self-realizing or self-information processing of the ultimate source. This is why positive always wins out over negative — because it is toward the source, whereas negative is always in the wrong direction, back toward nothingness. And suppose this process does extend beyond our dimension of space and time — then positive transcendence beyond this physical reality appears inevitable.

SPIRITUAL LEVEL OF BEING

As already mentioned, some people imagine that the universe is a lucky consequence of a sequence of lucky events, implying that there is no meaning to anything and that we are void of any direction, point, or purpose. But many other people, including myself, think this is nonsense. As I have postulated throughout this book, in trying to comprehend the ultimate reason for the universe, we have been brought face to face with an infinite source. So the creative potential of this source must also be infinite. It might be true that the universe is ascending up from nothing, and therefore, from this direction, has no potential for any bigger picture purpose. But if the universe is also **descending** from an infinite source, then we cannot be limited in our thinking regarding how much potential for purpose there is.

But without a medium to mediate this process, it would be impossible to decipher any distinction between either side, which could be likened to suggesting there is no difference between positive and negative. But positive is the natural opposite of negative, and these opposites create differentiation. The universe is this differential, or it is that which provides distinction between the two sides. Again, this is how the infinite positive side is self-realizing in relation to the negative side. Now, both sides can reconcile as a focused layer between both directions of potential. We, of course, are part of this focused layer. How can this be void of meaning? It has meaning of infinite magnitude.

Nature must gauge positive from negative, what works and what doesn't. This is necessary right down to the tiniest scales. Even what we might think of as inanimate matter is abuzz with energetic interactions at molecular, atomic, and subatomic scales. If particles and atoms are not interacting, they are (again, according to quantum physics) just non-physical waves of pure potential.

All this energetic work evolves through time to profound levels. And as we know, the universe has developed this process to the highly engaged focus we call life. Life itself then evolves to the status of sentient, even intelligent consciousness. I propose that it is through life that the ultimate source is more thoroughly self-unfolding, or self-realizing, by branching out with concentrations of interactive feedback. And again, this is the macro mind focused down to micro personal minds. And of course, we are again now talking in terms of the spiritual.

This inspirited source of our being is not only in our awareness or consciousness, it is in the inwardly focused subconscious part of our being. This is what keeps us alive, as exemplified by, for instance, the motor functions of the heart, immune system, etc. We do not need to be aware of this inward focus as the evolved unconscious takes care of that side of our being alive. This leaves the workings of our conscious mind and our feelings and senses free to experience. Both sides are just as much a part of being alive, but the surface ego part is only a brief expression of a deeper ethereal element.

I believe this deeper non-physical vitality is the spiritual level of our being, which is growing and expanding toward its ultimate nature through the medium of life. This underlying core level of our existence can never be viewed under a microscope or reduced to any mathematical equation or empirical observation: nothing **infinite** ever can.

FREE WILL

So, instead of the traditional view that we are physically developing a spiritual existence (bottom-up), I believe we are spiritually developing a physical existence (top-down). The spirit is the source of the universe reduced to the life force self-realizing as the soul. Consciousness is the interactive or sensory information feedback of the soul.

An essential property of the soul is that it has free will. Free will is the freedom of the micro mind within the macro or universal mind. The soul is free because it is part of the infinite possibilities of the ultimate source. This unfolding process is time. But, just as the speed of light slows time to a stop, so the ultimate source is not bound by time. The argument goes that, from the viewpoint of the source of the universe, the entire timeline of all creation is an ever-present "now" rather than a linear step-by-step progression. From this top-down perspective, space, time, and matter are comprehended in their entirety. In other words, the past, present, and future are not sequential but an interconnected coexistence — or looking forward in time is just the same as looking backward in time to the Creator of time.

Perhaps the infinite source needs time as part of its self-realization, even if the source itself is beyond this construct. From this "timelessness" perspective, the source would perceive the entire causal chain without the constraints of sequential order. Instead, it would see all cause and effect as a single, unified process. And from this viewpoint, the source could be considered omniscient and omnipresent. Many spiritual and philosophical traditions propose the idea of an "eternal now," where the deepest level of reality is an ever-present timeless moment. If true, the infinite source exists as this eternal now, where linear time is a mere illusion. This idea is made credible by science when considering *time dilation*. As Einstein himself put it: "The distinction between the past, present, and future is only a stubbornly persistent illusion."

Therefore, from the infinite source side looking down, time is predetermined because, from this perspective, all time, or the unfolding of creation, is contained within the infinite source. But looking up from the nothingness side, we have free will because we are part of the self-realizing of this infinite source through time. And so, from the viewpoint of the nothingness side, everything is yet to be determined, including our own free will. But from the viewpoint of the Infinite, the past, present, and future are all an expression of pure infinite potential. But because of mindfulness, memory, and the enlightenment of the soul, it is all far from meaningless — even if this is on a level far beyond our understanding.

HIGHER DIMENSIONS

It seems logical that the evolution of matter goes hand-in-hand with the evolution of consciousness. On a multi-dimensional scale, this evolution could transcend to higher planes of existence. Of course, we cannot conceive of what is possible, but the creative source is infinite in its potential to create, so this potential is limitless.

I believe that evolution is the "bringing to light" of the physical and the spiritual potential of the Infinite, perhaps for the benefit of higher realities or for higher dimensions of potential. The soul is part of this process, so it is part of what is being brought to light. In other words, the soul is a part of bringing pure potential into being by moving away from the negative nothingness and toward the light of the positive infiniteness (or "the Infinite").

There may be no limit to this potential, as there is no limit to the source from which we emerged. Perhaps consciousness is not just a part of universal awareness, but for the furtherance of spiritual growth. If by evolving away from the negative nothingness a soul can gravitate toward the Infinite, then we can reason that this continuance is ever toward a state of positive potential.

Hindus call it *Moksha*. Buddhists call it *Nirvana*. Christians call it *Heaven*. Whatever the name, these age-old beliefs appear to be saying the same thing: that is, the potential for self-awareness is to transcend toward a divine state of being. And it is through the emergence of pure being that the realization of value and meaning can emerge through experience. Now you can live. Now you can love. Now you can become and behold your true potential. This seems to be the measure and the meaning of our existence.

CONCLUSION

As you can see, by ***transcendence***, here, I mean to transcend spiritually. This involves the soul rising above the realm of this particular reality and moving on to a higher state of existence. I hope I have convinced you that it is not unrealistic to assume that the source of this universe can extend beyond the limitations of the narrow bandwidth of what we can see. And it is plausible to suggest that all levels of potential are part of a higher purpose, no matter how far beyond our understanding this may be.

In this book, I have tried to describe how the infinite first cause can only become less than infinite by being brought to light as more than nothing. All things are part of this dynamic process, including the bringing to light of our own spiritual soul. Perhaps the purpose of life is to demonstrate what this soul can or should be, and, just as importantly, what it should not.

All reality, I believe, exists due to the natural and inevitable conflict between the polar opposite fundamental starting points of the Infinite and the nothingness. But it is this battle that creates the formation of a front line. This is the energetic field of positive and negative interactive potential we know as the universe.

Much is stirred by this struggle, but it is this process that creates the realization of all things that are more than nothing, including our very own spiritual being as soldiers of the cause. We are a highly focused part of this naturally evolving process we know as nature and its infinitely positive potential to create **everything from nothing**.

And how could the first cause of all existence not be infinite compared to the opposite void of absolute nothingness? The ultimate source of our being is the antithesis of this void, drawing us back toward what age-old philosophical traditions worldwide have described as the divine abode of love, joy, and equanimity. Through the testimony of life, appreciation of this potential is awakened. This divine calling is to ascend to that from which we blindly descended but now blessed by the grace of the enlightenment we call the soul — the spiritual seat of our being.

Thank you for reading my book. I hope you enjoyed it. If so, all the years of research have been worthwhile. If you did find it interesting I would be forever grateful should you decide to leave a review at your online bookstore. Your opinion would not only be of interest to other potential readers but to myself too as the author. I read all reviews and would love to hear your thoughts. Thank you for your time.

About The Author

After more than three decades of research, philosopher and author of *Everything From Nothing*, S. E. Elwell, has refined his passion for the challenge of consolidating scientific, metaphysical, and philosophical insights. His writing is the result of researching common ground between these fields while staying in line with the current best theories, knowledge, and understandings.

www.ingramcontent.com/pod-product-compliance
Lightning Source LLC
Chambersburg PA
CBHW020516030426

42337CB00011B/411